"Bring the Classics to Life"

KIDNAPPED

LEVEL 3

Series Designer
Philip J. Solimene

Editor
Deborah Tiersch-Allen

Long Island, N.Y.

Story Adaptor

Jacqueline Nightingale

Author

Robert Louis Stevenson

HISTORICAL BACKGROUND

By the year 1751, Scotland had become one with England. Some of the people from the Highlands of Scotland were unhappy. They wanted their own Stuart line of kings to rule; so they fought against England. The Highlanders were punished by the English king. The way of life of the Highland people: their clan ownership of lands, their dress, and even their bagpipe music, was being taken away by law.

Scotland could not stand together against what was really ruled by England. The Lowland people of Scotland did not feel the same way as the Highlanders. And there was fighting among the clans. The Highlanders and the family of the Stuart kings did not win.

This is only a small part of the history behind the setting of Robert Louis Stevenson's classic KIDNAPPED. It is also interesting to note that the last name of the young man in the book, Balfour, was Stevenson's mother's family name.

Printed in U.S.A.
ISBN 0-931334-65-9

CONTENTS

WORDS USED

Story 21	Story 22	Story 23	Story 24	Story 25
KEY WORDS				
behave	correct	amaze	bargain	astonished
example	curious	beard	deserve	beauty
knight	deaf	camera	fortune	cardboard
squeeze	dumb	jewelry	keeper	cereal
stray	press	necklace	pitcher	flap
temper	rapidly	paste	season	heavens
NECESSARY WORDS				
	lightning	pirate	clan	belly
	thunder	soldier	mast	isle
	slave	roundhouse	reef	islet
			sword	starving
				tide

WORDS USED

Story 26	Story 27	Story 28	Story 29	Story 30
KEY WORDS				
birth	bedroom	coward	complain	average
cozy	brick	faithful	content	butcher
divide	clothing	gaze	greedy	copy
simple	lovely	impossible	message	loft
switch	note	inquire	recognize	pitch
willing	twice	sore	route	selfish
NECESSARY WORDS				
lad	heather			admire
	jail			kidnap
				tale

I Go to the House of Shaws

PREPARATION

Key Words

behave   (bi hāv′)   do what is the right thing
Be sure you <u>behave</u> at the show.
act in a special way
Mom wanted the children to <u>behave</u> nicely when they visited Grandmother.

example   (ig zam′ pəl)   a model
The pine tree is a good <u>example</u> of trees that stay green all year.

knight   (nīt)   a man who acted bravely and served in his king's army
The princess was rescued by the king's <u>knight</u>.

squeeze   (skwēz)   push hard
Mary wanted to <u>squeeze</u> an orange for juice.
force a way
Father had to <u>squeeze</u> through the crowd to get on the train.

stray   (strā)   lose one's way; wander
The babysitter watched the children carefully so they wouldn't <u>stray</u> from her in the park.
wandering
The <u>stray</u> dog was found and returned to its owner.

temper   (tem′ pə r)   state of mind or feelings
Because of Harry's bad <u>temper</u>, he didn't have any friends.

I Go to the House of Shaws

People

David Balfour   is a young man of seventeen who is telling the story of his adventures in Scotland.

Alexander Balfour   was David's father and Ebenezer's brother. He died a few months before David left on his journey.

Ebenezer Balfour   is David's uncle and Alexander's brother. He lives in the house of Shaws.

Mr. Campbell   is the minister of Essendean, Scotland, David's home town.

Places

Scotland   is part of Great Britain. It is north of England. Scotland is the home of the Scottish people. (Great Britain is made up of England, Scotland and Wales.)

Essendean   is a country town in the Lowlands of Scotland.

Edinburgh   is the capital city of Scotland.

Cramond   is a district in Scotland near the city of Edinburgh. This is where the house of Shaws was found.

I Go to the House of Shaws

A man with a gun came to the window and David told him about the letter he carried.

Preview:
1. Read the name of the story.
2. Look at the picture.
3. Read the sentence under the picture.
4. Read the first four paragraphs of the story.
5. Then answer the following question.

You learned from your preview that
_____a. David had visited his uncle Ebenezer at the house of Shaws many times before.
_____b. David did not know he belonged to the house of Shaws until Mr. Campbell told him.
_____c. David was going to live with Mr. Campbell, the minister.
_____d. David would go back to Essendean the very next day.

Turn to the Comprehension Check on page 10 for the right answer.

Now read the story.

Read to find out what David finds at the house of Shaws.

I Go to the House of Shaws

I will begin the story of my adventures with a morning early in June of 1751. I closed the door of my home in Essendean, Scotland for the last time. At the age of seventeen, I stood ready to find a new home.

My mother had been dead for a number of years. My father was dead only a few months. Mr. Campbell, the minister of the town church, walked with me to the river. He handed me a letter that my father had written.

"You must take this letter to the house of Shaws near Cramond," said Mr. Campbell. "Give it to your uncle, Ebenezer Balfour."

My name being David Balfour, I was now to know my true family background. The Shaws were an old rich Scottish family. I wondered what my poor schoolmaster father had to do with the house of Shaws.

Mr. Campbell gave me a small bag. In it was a Bible and some money. He told me to behave and show a good example of my country ways.

We said a sad good-bye. Then, with a squeeze of my arm, he turned and walked quickly away. I walked on. I did not feel like a lost stray boy. I felt like a knight charging ahead to meet things I did not yet know.

At the end of two days, I stopped walking at the top of a hill. My country home was far behind me. I looked down with wonder at the great sea and the capital city of Scotland, Edinburgh.

As I went along my way, I asked people about the great house of Shaws. At the sound of the name, each person got a strange look on his face. Finally, I met an old woman and asked her for directions. She was in a bad temper as she pointed the way. I began to wonder what strange things waited for me there.

At the top of a small hill, I sat down and stared at the house that would be my new home. It was not the great house I had hoped it would be. There was very little light inside, and no road led up to it. Many of the windows had no glass, and bats flew in and out.

I walked down and passed through the unfinished gates. The top floors of the house were open. They had never been completed. Steps to nowhere showed against the sky.

It was getting dark when I knocked on the door. I could hear that someone was in there, and I could see a fire. Still, no one answered. I wanted to run away, but my temper got the best of me. I knocked harder and began to shout.

Suddenly, I heard a man's voice above me and I looked up into the end of his gun. I told him about the letter I carried. The man left his stand at the window and came down. He opened the big piece of wood that was the door. Then he stared at me long and hard.

He was a mean, old-looking man in torn clothes. I followed him into the kitchen. There were locks on the closet doors, and his small supper was set on the table.

The man shared his poor meal with me. Then he cried, "Give me my brother Alexander's letter!"

I was surprised when he said he was my uncle. But I was more surprised to hear he was my father's brother. Uncle Ebenezer was surely not the great knight I thought he would be. And the big house of Shaws was not a good example of what riches might buy. It was a cold, dark, empty place.

When it became late, my uncle led me up the stairs and down a dark hall to my room. He carried no light. As I walked into the dark room, he closed and locked the door behind me. I wanted to cry, but I was too tired to squeeze out the tears.

This was not the way I thought my uncle would behave. I wondered if this was an example of how my life here would be.

My room was cold and my bed was damp. I put my woolen cloth on the floor, wrapped myself up, and went to sleep.

I Go to the House of Shaws

COMPREHENSION CHECK

Preview Answer:

b. David did not know he belonged to the house of Shaws until Mr. Campbell told him.

Choose the best answer.

1. This story takes place in the country of
   ____a. America.
   ____b. Scotland.
   ____c. England.
   ____d. Mexico.

2. When David Balfour left his home in Essendean, he was
   ____a. ten years old.
   ____b. fourteen years old.
   ____c. seventeen years old.
   ____d. seven years old.

3. In the beginning of the story, David was
   ____a. excited about his new life.
   ____b. afraid to leave his home.
   ____c. angry at being one of the Shaws.
   ____d. mean to Mr. Campbell.

4. David's father, Alexander, was
   ____a. a town minister in Essendean.
   ____b. a rich man in Essendean.
   ____c. a king in Essendean.
   ____d. a poor schoolmaster in Essendean.

5. When David came to the house of Shaws,
   ____a. he was happy about what he found.
   ____b. he was disappointed at what he saw.
   ____c. he was ready to take over.
   ____d. he was told that his uncle was dead.

6. Uncle Ebenezer
   ____a. seemed to like visitors.
   ____b. was glad to see David.
   ____c. didn't seem to trust anyone.
   ____d. treated David very well.

7. The house of Shaws was
   ____a. filled with pretty things.
   ____b. in a very poor way.
   ____c. finished a long time ago.
   ____d. going to be sold very soon.

8. Ebenezer Balfour
   ____a. lived in great riches and happiness.
   ____b. lived with his wife and children.
   ____c. lived only to see his brother.
   ____d. lived the life of a poor man.

9. Another name for this story could be
   ____a. "The Understanding Minister."
   ____b. "Life in the City of Edinburgh."
   ____c. "Meeting a Fine and Loving Uncle."
   ____d. "The Surprise at the End of the Journey."

10. This story is mainly about
    ____a. an old rich man who gives away money.
    ____b. a young man beginning a new life.
    ____c. a minister in a town in Scotland.
    ____d. a father who misses his son.

Check your answers with the key on page 68.

I Go to the House of Shaws

VOCABULARY CHECK

behave	example	knight	squeeze	stray	temper

I. Sentences to Finish

Fill in the blank in each sentence with the correct key word from the box above.

1. The _____ wore a suit of shiny metal called armor.

2. After the accident, Carol was in a terrible _____ .

3. The teacher showed the children an _____ of a friendly letter and asked them to write one of their own.

4. You have to _____ the tube to get the toothpaste out.

5. The children were allowed to go to the movies, after they promised to stay in their seats and _____ .

6. We put a fence around our yard so our dog would not _____ .

II. Crossword Puzzle

Fill in the puzzle with the key words from the box above. Use the meanings below to help you choose the right word.

Across

1. a man who served in the king's army

3. a model

4. push hard

5. act in a special way

Down

2. state of mind or feelings

4. wander

Check your answers with the key on page 69.

This page may be reproduced for classroom use.

I Find Myself in Danger

PREPARATION

Key Words

correct	(kə rekt′)	right; without mistakes *Father showed Peggy the <u>correct</u> way to use a saw.*
curious	(kyur′e əs)	eager to know or learn *Jeff was <u>curious</u> to learn how the engine worked.* strange looking; unusual *There was a <u>curious</u> old lamp in Grandmother's house.*
deaf	(def)	not able to hear *The doctors tried hard to make the <u>deaf</u> boy hear again.*
dumb	(dum)	stupid; foolish *It was <u>dumb</u> to cross the street without looking both ways.* not able to speak *Today, many <u>dumb</u> children can be taught to speak in sign language.*
press	(pres)	push against; squeeze; force *<u>Press</u> hard on the pen and it should write.*
rapidly	(rap′ id lē)	quickly *Rita dressed <u>rapidly</u> so she wouldn't be late for school.*

I Find Myself in Danger

Necessary Words

lightning   (līt ′ ning)   flash of light in the sky usually seen during a storm
The lightning lit up the sky for miles.

thunder   (thun ′ d ər)   a loud noise that goes with or follows lightning
The thunder was so loud that it shook the house.

slave   (slāv)   a person who belongs to another
If David became a slave, he would have to pick cotton in the fields.

People

Ransome   is a young cabin boy on the ship Covenant.

Captain Hoseason   is the captain of the ship Covenant.

Mr. Rankeillor   is the lawyer of the town of Queensferry, Scotland.

Places

Queensferry   is a town in Scotland near Edinburgh. It lies on the place where the Firth of Forth narrows into a river. (See ⑩ on map, page 67.)

the Queen's Ferry   is a place on the narrow part of the Firth of Forth in Scotland where boats carry people and goods across to the other shore.

Things

Covenant   is a trading ship anchored near the Queen's Ferry. It has two masts that hold square sails.

cabin boy   is a boy or man who works on a ship, waiting on or taking care of the needs of the officers and passengers.

I Find Myself in Danger

David was full of anger and fear when he saw where his uncle had sent him.

Preview:
1. Read the name of the story.
2. Look at the picture.
3. Read the sentence under the picture.
4. Read the first three paragraphs of the story.
5. Then answer the following question.

You learned from your preview that
____a. David's father, Alexander, was not Ebenezer's brother.
____b. something was not right at the house of Shaws.
____c. David was happy to be at the house of Shaws.
____d. there were no books in Ebenezer's house.

Turn to the Comprehension Check on page 16 for the right answer.

Now read the story.

Read to find out how David is in danger.

I Find Myself in Danger

The next morning, I shouted until my uncle opened the door. From the way my uncle behaved, I knew he did not like me. He wished I had never come. And I was thinking the very same thoughts myself.

After lunch, my uncle led me to a room with many books. I was a curious person, so I sat down to read. In one of the books I found some words written in my father's handwriting. They read, *"To my brother Ebenezer on his fifth birthday."*

I thought this was most curious. Uncle Ebenezer had come to own this house because he was the oldest son. These words meant that my father must have known how to write before the age of five. Perhaps my father had been the oldest.

I spoke to my uncle about this. First, he got very angry. Then he turned a deaf ear to me. He said he did not want to speak about my father.

Suddenly, I felt Uncle Ebenezer press some gold pieces into my hand. I was struck dumb by his sudden eagerness to share his money. He said he wanted me to help him by doing small jobs around the house.

My uncle sent me to the far end of the house. He told me to climb to the top of the tower and bring down a chest. I was to stay close to the wall because there was nothing to hold on to.

My uncle would not let me use a light, so I got on my hands and knees and felt my way. It was dark inside the tower. My heart beat rapidly as I climbed the five sets of steps to the top.

I had almost reached the top, when there was a sudden flash of lightning. I saw the sky all around me! The tower had never been finished. One more step and I would have fallen to my death.

A sudden crash of thunder made a roaring noise. I was full of anger and fear as I climbed down the steps. I found my uncle drinking in the kitchen. I came up behind him and grabbed him.

Uncle Ebenezer was very frightened at seeing me alive. He fell to the floor. He was too sick to talk and he went to bed. I locked him in his room.

The next morning at breakfast, I started to press my uncle to give some correct answers to my questions. But there came a knock at the door. I quickly jumped up to answer it. Before me stood a young boy in sea clothes. He had a letter for my uncle from Captain Hoseason. The captain was from the trading ship called the Covenant.

My uncle read the letter and said he had to see the Captain. I was to go along to the Queen's Ferry. After seeing the Captain, we would call on Mr. Rankeillor, the lawyer of the town of Queensferry. Mr. Rankeillor knew my father. I said I would go. I thought no harm would come to me with people all around.

As we walked, I talked to Ransome. He worked on the Covenant as cabin boy. He had many good and bad stories to tell about the ship. He said that some men were taken on board, brought to America and sold for slaves.

We came to the top of the hill that looked over the sea. My heart beat rapidly as I looked at the Covenant. I told myself I would never get on board that ship.

At the inn, I left my uncle with Captain Hoseason. A man downstairs told me that people thought Ebenezer had killed his older brother, Alexander. I was correct in thinking that my father had been the oldest. Now, everything really belonged to me.

The Captain took me out to the Covenant in a small boat. He whispered that I must be careful of my uncle. I thought the Captain was my friend. The Captain and I went on board the Covenant first. When I turned around, my uncle was headed away from the ship.

How could I have been so dumb? I cried out, but my uncle turned a deaf ear to me. Suddenly, I saw a flash of light and I fell into darkness.

I Find Myself in Danger

COMPREHENSION CHECK

Choose the best answer.

1. David and his uncle
   _____a. were glad to be together.
   _____b. liked to talk about David's father.
   _____c. did not like each other.
   _____d. were very much alike in some ways.

2. From the way David Balfour thinks and acts, you know that
   _____a. he is a fresh boy from the country.
   _____b. he does not want to help his uncle.
   _____c. he is a smart young man and a nice one.
   _____d. he wants only his uncle's money.

3. Ebenezer Balfour
   _____a. did not want to share anything with David.
   _____b. wanted David to keep him company.
   _____c. did not want David to get hurt.
   _____d. gave David what belonged to him right away.

4. The Covenant was
   _____a. a trading ship.
   _____b. a special letter.
   _____c. a house in Scotland.
   _____d. a family name.

5. Which **two** of the following are true about David's father, Alexander Balfour?
   _____a. He was thought to have been killed by Ebenezer.
   _____b. He was the oldest brother of Shaws.
   _____c. He was not known by any people David met.
   _____d. He was much younger than Ebenezer.

6. At the inn,
   _____a. David found out that Uncle Ebenezer was a nice man.
   _____b. David stayed and met with his uncle and the captain.
   _____c. David learned that there was more to the story of the Shaws than his uncle was telling.
   _____d. David decided to sail on the ship Covenant with his new friend Ransome.

7. Uncle Ebenezer
   _____a. wanted David to be happy.
   _____b. was a man that had many nice friends.
   _____c. wanted to send David on a fun vacation.
   _____d. was a cold, mean man.

8. Captain Hoseason
   _____a. really felt sorry for David Balfour.
   _____b. was not a friend of Ebenezer's.
   _____c. just wanted to show David his ship.
   _____d. made David believe he could be trusted.

9. Another name for this story could be
   _____a. "Meeting a Friendly Captain."
   _____b. "Trouble for David Balfour."
   _____c. "A Visit to Mr. Rankeillor."
   _____d. "Learning to Sail a Ship."

10. This story is mainly about
   _____a. how David's uncle tries to get rid of him.
   _____b. how David makes some new friends.
   _____c. how David fights back against his uncle.
   _____d. how David takes care of young Ransome.

Check your answers with the key on page 68.

This page may be reproduced for classroom use.

I Find Myself in Danger

VOCABULARY CHECK

| correct | curious | deaf | dumb | press | rapidly |

I. Sentences to Finish

Fill in the blank in each sentence with the correct key word from the box above.

1. The water ran _____ down the falls.

2. I was _____ about how boats were made, so I read a book about ship-building.

3. Sally had to _____ the doorbell many times before someone answered.

4. I was struck _____ when Andy said he would not give me a ride back to town.

5. Susan checked her answers with the _____ ones on the back of the paper.

6. I called to the young boy many times before I found out he was _____ and could not hear me.

II. Word Search

All the words from the box above are hidden in the puzzle below. As you find each word, put a circle around it. One word, that is not a key word, has been done for you.

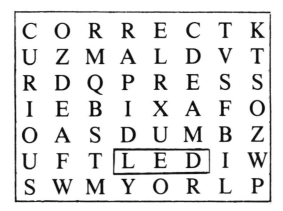

```
C O R R E C T K
U Z M A L D V T
R D Q P R E S S
I E B I X A F O
O A S D U M B Z
U F T [L E D] I W
S W M Y O R L P
```

Check your answers with the key on page 69.

This page may be reproduced for classroom use.

The Ship Called Covenant

PREPARATION

Key Words

amaze   (ə māz ′)   to cause wonder
It would <u>amaze</u> you to see how much weight she lost.

beard   (bērd)   hair growing on a man's face
It took Larry four months to grow his <u>beard</u>.

camera   (kam ′ ər ə)   a machine for taking pictures
We used a <u>camera</u> to take pictures of our dog.

jewelry   (jü ′ əl rē)   a group or set of jewels, usually worth a lot of money
It is wise to keep good <u>jewelry</u> in a safe place.

necklace   (nek ′ lis)   a string of jewels or beads worn around the neck
Phil gave Vicky a gold <u>necklace</u> for her birthday.

paste   (pāst)   a mix to stick paper together
I used <u>paste</u> to put the pieces of my picture together.

to stick two things together
Barney wanted to <u>paste</u> his pictures in a large book.

The Ship Called Covenant

Necessary Words

pirate   (pī ′ rit)   a person who attacks and steals from ships

The pirate took all the gold off the ship and shared it with his friends.

soldier   (sōl ′ jər)   a man who serves in the army
The soldier fought bravely for his country.

roundhouse   (round ′ hous)   a cabin in the back part of a ship
Captain Hoseason, Mr. Riach and Mr. Shaun slept and ate in the roundhouse on the Covenant.

People

Mr. Riach   is second to the captain in charge of the ship Covenant.

Mr. Shaun   is the chief sailor and second to the captain on the ship Covenant.

Alan Breck Stewart   is a passenger on the Covenant after his boat sinks. He is from Scotland, but he wears the coat of a French soldier.

Louis XV   was the king of France from 1715 to 1774.

George II   was the king of England from 1727 to 1760.

Places

England   is the largest part of Great Britain. It is in the southern part.

France   is a country in western Europe.

The Ship Called Covenant

The next time I woke up, there was a man standing over me with a light. He cared for my cuts and gave me a drink.

Preview:
1. Read the name of the story.
2. Look at the picture.
3. Read the sentences under the picture.
4. Read the first two paragraphs of the story.
5. Then answer the following question.

You learned from your preview that
____a. David had a warm feeling about his uncle.
____b. David was alone on the ship.
____c. David had returned to the house of Shaws.
____d. David was being held on the Covenant.

Turn to the Comprehension Check on page 22 for the right answer.

Now read the story.

Read to find out if David will escape.

The Ship Called Covenant

I woke up in darkness. My body hurt all over, and my head was spinning. The repeated rolling of the ship in the ocean, and my growing hatred for my uncle, led me back into a long sleep.

When I came to myself again, a small man of about thirty was standing over me with a light. He had green eyes and a beard. He asked me if I had eaten. I said the thought of meat made me more sick. My mouth felt like it was full of paste. The green-eyed man gave me a drink. Then he washed and covered the cuts on my head, and went away.

A short time later, the man with the beard came back. He brought the Captain with him.

"The boy is ill and has not eaten. I want him brought up front right away," said the man.

"Do as you please, Riach," answered the Captain. "I have no use for the boy right now."

My ropes were cut and I was taken to the place where the sailors lived. It was good to see daylight after so long in the dark. I lay in my bed for many days. Sleep, good food, and the sailor's care made me healthy again.

The sailors of the Covenant were a hard group of men. Some had been pirates on the high seas. Others had left the ships of their kings and were wanted by the law. But I was amazed at how kind they were to me.

When I was well again, the sailors returned my money to me. I think I would have taken a picture to remember them by if there had been cameras in my time.

Ransome came to visit me often. Many times he would be caring for a bad leg or a cut given to him by Mr. Shaun, the chief sailor. Mr. Shaun liked to drink.

I learned from Ransome that the ship was headed for the United States. I was going to be sold as a slave.

One night, my blood ran cold as I saw two men carrying Ransome. His color was as white as paste. He was dead. Ransome had brought Mr. Shaun a dirty cup. For this, Mr. Shaun had killed the boy. I knew, then, that I had more to fear on this ship than just the captain.

I had to do Ransome's job in the roundhouse. It was not so bad when I could forget my fears. The food was tasty enough. And as long as I did my work, all was well. But the shadow of poor Ransome stood heavy around all of us. The camera in my mind kept his picture alive.

A fair week of work had gone by. It was night, and a thick white blanket of fog hung around the ship. Suddenly, we heard a loud noise.

"We've run a boat down," shouted the Captain.

Only one of the passengers on the wrecked boat was saved. Captain Hoseason helped the man on board. The captain stared long and hard at the man's fine clothes. He looked at the man's jewelry, especially his gold necklace.

After the man ate, he removed his necklace and his money belt. He put them on the table. The Captain eyed them for a time.

When the Captain left the cabin, the man talked to me freely. The man was from Scotland, but he was against King George II. He had served King Louis XV of France. This man would be in danger from King George's soldiers as soon as he set foot on land.

I left the new passenger to get him something to drink. I heard the Captain and Riach making plans to take his money belt and jewelry. I was angry and frightened, but I managed to get the key to the box where the guns were kept. I went back to the man with some guns.

I told the man of the Captain's plans. He told me his name was Alan Breck Stewart. Together, Alan and I made our plan to take over the Covenant. I was amazed at his courage. Finally, I had hope in the name of Alan Breck.

The Ship Called Covenant

COMPREHENSION CHECK

Choose the best answer.

1. Mr. Riach and the sailors
   ____a. were very mean to David.
   ____b. helped David get well.
   ____c. were nice in all things.
   ____d. were all from the king's army.

2. Uncle Ebenezer put David on the Covenant because
   ____a. he thought David should learn how to sail.
   ____b. he wanted to take a trip himself.
   ____c. he had arranged for David to be sold as a slave.
   ____d. he liked David and wanted him to have friends.

3. Alan Breck Stewart came on board when
   ____a. his ship was run over by the Covenant.
   ____b. he called to the Captain from the shore.
   ____c. the Covenant stopped to pick up sailors.
   ____d. David was brought on at the Queen's Ferry.

4. Mr. Shaun, the chief sailor,
   ____a. was a nice, quiet man who helped David.
   ____b. cared a lot about Ransome.
   ____c. did not scare David at all.
   ____d. was a mean man who liked to drink.

5. After Ransome's death,
   ____a. David worked in the roundhouse as cabin boy.
   ____b. Mr. Shaun was thrown into the sea.
   ____c. David would not take orders from anyone.
   ____d. Mr. Shaun let David off the ship.

6. Alan Breck was from
   ____a. France.
   ____b. England.
   ____c. America.
   ____d. Scotland.

7. David Balfour
   ____a. was not able to think quickly in times of trouble.
   ____b. felt very strongly that what the Captain and Riach were planning to do to Alan Breck was wrong.
   ____c. did not want to stand against the Captain and the other sailors on the Covenant.
   ____d. felt he could not believe in Alan Breck.

8. David and Alan
   ____a. did not think a plan was necessary.
   ____b. should not have taken the guns.
   ____c. would have been better off without each other.
   ____d. helped and trusted one another.

9. Another name for this story could be
   ____a. "The Man with the Green Eyes."
   ____b. "Adventures On Board the Covenant."
   ____c. "Uncle Ebenezer's Riches."
   ____d. "Living Through a Shipwreck."

10. This story is mainly about
    ____a. how Uncle Ebenezer makes a deal with Captain Hoseason.
    ____b. how Ransome brings a dirty cup and is killed by Mr. Shaun.
    ____c. how Alan Breck Stewart fought against King George II.
    ____d. how David handles the people and the happenings on the Covenant.

Check your answers with the key on page 68.

This page may be reproduced for classroom use.

The Ship Called Covenant

VOCABULARY CHECK

amaze	beard	camera	jewelry	necklace	paste

I. Sentences to Finish

Fill in the blank in each sentence with the correct key word from the box above.

1. Karen used special _____ to put up the wallpaper in the kitchen.

2. The tricks at the magic show will _____ you.

3. Anne liked _____ , so she always wore many rings and bracelets.

4. I used my _____ to take a picture of the beautiful sunset.

5. John grew a _____ , so he did not shave for a few months.

6. I gave Sharon a gold _____ for her birthday.

II. Matching

Write the letter of the correct meaning from Column B next to the key word in Column A.

Column A	Column B
____ 1. necklace	a. a group of jewels
____ 2. beard	b. a mix to stick paper together
____ 3. camera	c. to cause to wonder
____ 4. amaze	d. a machine for taking pictures
____ 5. jewelry	e. hair growing on a man's face
____ 6. paste	f. a string of jewels worn around the neck

Check your answers with the key on page 69.

This page may be reproduced for classroom use.

I Join With Alan Breck Stewart

PREPARATION

Key Words

bargain	(bär ´ gən)	something that is bought at a very good price *Two candy bars for the price of one is a bargain.* an understanding between people *The bargain called for us to give Sam food and he would give us water.*
deserve	(di zėrv ´)	to earn or to have a right to *We often get what we deserve.*
fortune	(fôr ´ chən)	money or other riches *She made a fortune selling her paintings.* luck or chance *It was our good fortune to meet with friendly people along life's way.*
keeper	(kē ´ pər)	a person who takes care of an animal someone who owns a store or shop one who has and takes care of something *Susan was the keeper of the plants.*
pitcher	(pich ´ ər)	someone who throws a ball something to hold liquids, with a lip for pouring *Mother poured milk from the pitcher.*
season	(sē ´ zn)	one of the times of year: spring, summer, autumn, or winter *People who like snow enjoy the winter season.*

I Join With Alan Breck Stewart

Necessary Words

clan	(klan)	a group of families that are born from the same parents, grandparents, great-grandparents, and so on. *Alan's <u>clan</u> lived in Appin, Scotland.*
mast	(mast)	a tall pole coming up from the bottom of a ship and rising high into the air to hold the sails and ropes *A large, square sail hung from the <u>mast</u> of the passing ship.*
reef	(rēf)	a narrow strip of rocks near the top of the water *The ship hit a <u>reef</u> and sunk to the bottom of the sea.*
sword	(sôrd, sōrd)	a long, sharp, metal blade that is set in a handle, used for fighting *The soldier pulled out his <u>sword</u> and charged the enemy.*

Places

Glasgow	is the main seaport and largest city in Scotland. It is on the Clyde River.
Highlands	a mountainous part in north and west Scotland
Lowlands	a low, flat part in south and east Scotland

I Join With Alan Breck Stewart

Alan and I were ready to meet the Captain and the sailors in the roundhouse.

Preview:
1. Read the name of the story.
2. Look at the picture.
3. Read the sentence under the picture.
4. Read the first three paragraphs of the story.
5. Then answer the following question.

You learned from your preview that
_____a. there was going to be a fight on the Covenant.
_____b. David would not fight against the Captain.
_____c. Alan Breck was going to be keeper of the guns.
_____d. the Captain understood why David was going to fight.

Turn to the Comprehension Check on page 28 for the right answer.

Now read the story.

Read to find out who will win the fight.

I Join With Alan Breck Stewart

Alan and I got ready for our attack from the round-house. Alan stood in the door-way with his sword in hand. I watched over the window and was keeper of the guns.

Captain Hoseason appeared in the doorway. He frowned at Alan and looked over in my direction. "David," he said, "I will remember this." A lump formed in my throat.

We heard the Captain whispering to the men. And we knew they were starting their attack on the roundhouse. Suddenly, Mr. Shaun came to the door.

"That's him that killed poor Ransome," I shouted.

"Look to your window!" cried Alan. And Mr. Shaun was dead by Alan's sword.

I had never fired a gun before, but it was now or never. The shots that followed were deafening. The roundhouse was filled with smoke. I looked over at Alan's sword and I knew that Alan Breck Stewart was a fighter. The men that came before him fell one and then another.

"They're getting what they deserve," I thought to myself.

Suddenly, everything was silent. Dead men lay all around us. Alan was so happy that he hugged me.

"Am I not a good fighter?" he asked, his eyes bright and his face red.

When I came to understand the meaning of all this, I started to cry. Alan said I needed some sleep, so he guarded the cabin first.

Mr. Riach and the Captain took turns steering the ship. Many of the other sailors had been hurt or killed. Alan and I sat at the table in the round-house. We shared a pitcher of drink. It was our good fortune to find the best food and drink on the ship within our reach.

Alan took one of the silver buttons off his fine coat and gave it to me. He said the silver buttons had belonged to his father. I was to show the button wherever I went. The friends of Alan Breck would know I, too, was a friend and they would help me. When I left the ship, this would be part of my small fortune. I was proud to be the keeper of it.

Soon, the Captain wanted to make a bargain with us. We said he could come to the window and talk. The Captain wanted to go to Glasgow to get more sailors, but Alan would not hear of it.

The Captain finally said he would let Alan off the ship near the country of his people in the Highlands. Alan needed the help of his clan. Then we gave the Captain and Mr. Riach some drink, and they gave us some water. That was the last part of the bargain.

Alan and I sat for hours drinking from the pitcher. He told me his stories and I told him mine. But when I came to the part about Mr. Campbell the minister, Alan cried out. Alan thought I was fine, even though he usually didn't like Lowlanders. But he really did not like any person by the name of Campbell. He said that the Campbells had cheated the Stewarts out of their lands for many a season.

Alan had left Scotland and gone to France. I could not understand why he wanted to come back to face such danger. But he said he missed his home of Appin and his friends as well. Alan told me about a man with bright red hair called the Red Fox. The Red Fox was really Colin Roy Campbell, and Colin was no friend to Alan's people in Appin.

The Captain said there was trouble on deck. Alan and I went up to see what was wrong. The wind was blowing hard, and there were reefs here and there in the water.

The Captain was afraid for his ship and he had every right. Suddenly, we hit one of the reefs. I was thrown into the deep water.

I was beginning to think my life was lost for good, when I grabbed hold of a mast that was floating by. I was not much of a swimmer, but I kicked and splashed for about an hour. Though the season was summer, the water was cold. I was never so glad as when I finally landed upon a small island.

I Join With Alan Breck Stewart

COMPREHENSION CHECK

Choose the best answer.

Preview Answer:

a. there was going to be a fight on the Covenant.

1. David and Alan
   ____a. lost the fight to the sailors.
   ____b. won the fight at the roundhouse.
   ____c. made the Captain get off the ship.
   ____d. did not like each other very much.

2. Alan Breck
   ____a. was not a very good fighter.
   ____b. was afraid of Captain Hoseason and the sailors.
   ____c. was pleased with his king, King George II.
   ____d. was proud of his people and the way he could fight.

3. As a sign that they were friends, Alan gave David
   ____a. a gold coin.
   ____b. a silver button.
   ____c. a silver necklace.
   ____d. a gold ring.

4. Alan Breck Stewart
   ____a. was a friend of all the Campbells.
   ____b. belonged to the group known as the Campbells.
   ____c. wanted to become one of the Campbells.
   ____d. did not like the Campbells at all.

5. The Red Fox was really
   ____a. Colin Roy Campbell.
   ____b. Alan Breck Stewart.
   ____c. David Balfour.
   ____d. Captain Hoseason.

6. Alan's clan lived in
   ____a. Queensferry.
   ____b. Glasgow.
   ____c. Appin.
   ____d. Essendean.

7. One of the reasons that the Covenant hit a reef could be
   ____a. there were not enough men left after the fight to sail her.
   ____b. the Captain wanted to sink the ship so David would get off.
   ____c. the ship had a big hole in the side.
   ____d. there was no wind to push the ship along.

8. By the end of the story,
   ____a. Alan Breck was tossed into the sea.
   ____b. David finds himself on a small island.
   ____c. Alan Breck and David are safe on the ship.
   ____d. David has drowned in the cold sea.

9. Another name for this story could be
   ____a. "A Sea Full of Reefs."
   ____b. "Alan's People in Appin."
   ____c. "I Must Fight to Stay Alive."
   ____d. "Fun on the Ship Covenant."

10. This story is mainly about
   ____a. how a young man finds out he cannot save himself from trouble.
   ____b. how David must be strong and do new things to save his own life.
   ____c. how good a fighter Alan Breck Stewart really is.
   ____d. how a ship sinks after a bad storm on the seas.

Check your answers with the key on page 68.

I Join With Alan Breck Stewart

VOCABULARY CHECK

bargain	deserve	fortune	keeper	pitcher	season

I. Sentences to Finish

Fill in the blank in each sentence with the correct key word from the box above.

1. Mr. Johnson is a _____ of bees, and he collects the honey from the beehives.

2. People who like to swim enjoy the summer _____ .

3. Mom poured a glass of juice from the _____ .

4. Sally got a real _____ when she bought a dress for half its usual price.

5. The rich man left his _____ to his only child.

6. After a long day at work or school, a person does _____ a rest.

II. Matching

Write the letter of the correct meaning from Column B next to the key word in Column A.

Column A	Column B
____ 1. fortune	a. to earn or have a right to
____ 2. season	b. a person who takes care of something
____ 3. deserve	c. someone who throws a ball
____ 4. keeper	d. money or other riches
____ 5. pitcher	e. something bought at a good price
____ 6. bargain	f. one of the times of the year

Check your answers with the key on page 70.

Through the Isle of Mull

PREPARATION

Key Words

astonished	(ə ston´ isht)	amazed *Harry was astonished to learn he had lost his job.*
beauty	(byü´ tē)	good looks; something beautiful *The mirror told the queen of Snow White's great beauty.*
cardboard	(kärd´ bôrd)	a stiff paper used to make cards and boxes *Paste a piece of cardboard behind the picture to keep it stiff.*
cereal	(sir´ ē əl)	a food made from grain *Juice, cereal, and milk make a good breakfast.*
flap	(flap)	a flat piece hanging or folded over something *Fold over the flap on the letter and write your return address on it.* to fly by moving wings up and down *The bird began to flap its wings.*
heavens	(hev´ ənz)	sky *The full moon lit up the heavens.*

Through the Isle of Mull

Necessary Words

belly	(bel ′ ē)	the lower part of the human body that contains the stomach and the intestines *After having no food for a long time, my belly began to hurt.*
isle	(īl)	island *We enjoyed beautiful weather on the sunny isle.*
islet	(ī ′ let)	small island *The islet disappeared as soon as the sea water got high.*
starving	(stärv ′ ing)	suffering from great hunger *The starving animal searched the burned woods for a sign of food.*
tide	(tīd)	the rising and falling of the waters of the ocean, usually happening about every twelve hours *When the tide went out, we could see a strip of sand in the ocean.*

Places

Earraid	is a tidal island off the coast of Mull. The Covenant hit a reef near Earraid. (See ① on map, page 67.)
Mull	is an island off the coast of Morven. (See ② on map, page 67.)
Morven	is a part of the mainland of Scotland in the western Highlands. (See ③ on map, page 67.)

Through the Isle of Mull

David climbed a hill and looked out over the sea for a sign of the Covenant.

Preview:
1. Read the name of the story.
2. Look at the picture.
3. Read the sentence under the picture.
4. Read the first three paragraphs of the story.
5. Then answer the following question.

You learned from your preview that
____a. the Covenant was only a short distance away.
____b. Alan Breck was on the island with David.
____c. people came to welcome David to the island.
____d. David was alone on a small island.

Turn to the Comprehension Check on page 34 for the right answer.

Now read the story.

Read to find out if David will ever get off the islet.

Through the Isle of Mull

I washed up on shore, and began the worst part of my adventures. I was wet and cold. To keep from freezing, I walked back and forth in the sand.

At dawn, I set out to look around the small island called Earraid. I climbed a hill, falling a good part of the way up. I looked out over the sea, but there was no sign of the Covenant.

I was so hungry by now that my belly hurt. I walked toward the east along the coast, hoping to find a house. But the only sign of life was a bird flapping its wings.

My travels were stopped by a creek that ran deep into the small island. I was not able to get across. I could see the main island of Mull, but I could not get to it.

I was feeling sorry for myself. It started raining and did not stop. I was cold and starving. After eating some shell fish from the sea, I became very sick. My mouth felt as dry as cardboard.

On my second day on the islet, there was more rain and sickness. I looked to the heavens and hoped that there would soon be an end to the wet weather.

As I crossed the islet, I found that no one part was better than another. To make matters worse, I discovered a hole in my money pocket. Most of my money had been lost.

By the third morning, my clothes were very worn. The flap on my shirt pocket hung by a thread. My throat was hurting badly and my body was as stiff as cardboard.

The rain finally stopped, and the sun was bright in the heavens. The sunshine gave even my small empty island some beauty.

From the top of a high rock, I saw a boat carrying two fishermen. They were near enough to hear me, so I shouted to them. They called out some words I did not understand, and laughed. I was astonished when they passed me by.

The next day, I was weak and feeling more sorry for myself. I had just gotten up on my rock when I saw the same boat coming back my way. The men shouted to me in words I did not know. They kept laughing as they spoke. The only word I could understand was the word tide. One man kept saying "tide" and waving toward the main island.

I went back to the creek. I was astonished to find that I could just walk across the creek when the tide was out. A country boy like myself did not even think of that. I had spent four terrible days on an empty islet when I could have walked right onto the main island.

I stepped onto the Isle of Mull. There were no roads I knew. But after a time, I came upon a house at the bottom of a hill. A kind man and his wife lived there. The man told me that some passengers from the wrecked Covenant had gotten to shore and stopped at his house.

Alan had left word for the boy with the silver button. I was to follow him to his part of the country by way of Toro-say. The good man and his wife invited me to supper, and I stayed the night. The bowl of cereal they set before me might as well have been a feast after what I had eaten on the islet.

After a good night's sleep and a breakfast of cereal, I was on my way again. I felt more fit than when I had arrived. I learned much about the Highlands that day. The people were very poor, but the land was a thing of beauty.

I followed roads I did not know. One man had to have money before giving me directions. Another man was blind and carried a gun. Finally, I met an innkeeper who was more well-off than most. He was friendly and offered me a room for the night.

I was feeling much better when I started my journey to the mainland of Morven. I had gone almost a hundred miles in four days.

Through the Isle of Mull

COMPREHENSION CHECK

Choose the best answer.

1. David got to the main island of Mull when
    ____a. the tide went out and the creek waters got low.
    ____b. the fishermen gave him a ride in their boat.
    ____c. they built a bridge from one island to another.
    ____d. Alan Breck came to help him swim across.

2. The fishermen had not stopped to help David the first time because
    ____a. they were mean men who didn't care about boys.
    ____b. they were friends of Ebenezer Balfour.
    ____c. they didn't understand why he couldn't get off the islet.
    ____d. they were having trouble with their boat and went to Mull.

3. David spent four days on the islet because
    ____a. he liked to eat shellfish.
    ____b. he enjoyed island weather.
    ____c. he was from the country and did not know about tides and the sea.
    ____d. he was sure that Alan Breck would come back and take him away.

4. David stayed alive on the empty islet
    ____a. by sleeping in a nice man's house.
    ____b. by eating the birds that nested there.
    ____c. by climbing to the top of a hill and looking around.
    ____d. by moving around to stay warm and eating shellfish.

5. Alan Breck Stewart
    ____a. waited at a house on Mull for David to get there.
    ____b. left word for David about how and where to find him.
    ____c. died in the wreck of the Covenant.
    ____d. told people to send David home.

6. Once he was on the Isle of Mull, David
    ____a. met all different kinds of people.
    ____b. slept in the woods all night.
    ____c. found Alan at a nearby house.
    ____d. thought he might go back to the islet.

7. Which **two** of the following were true about the Highlands as David tells it?
    ____a. The land was beautiful.
    ____b. The people were very rich.
    ____c. The land was empty and cold.
    ____d. The people were very poor.

8. In four days, David had travelled
    ____a. almost three hundred miles.
    ____b. more than two hundred miles.
    ____c. less than fifty miles.
    ____d. almost a hundred miles.

9. Another name for this story could be
    ____a. "I Become a Fisherman."
    ____b. "My Island Travels."
    ____c. "Living on a Sunny Island."
    ____d. "Alan Returns For Me."

10. This story is mainly about
    ____a. how David learns to talk with new people.
    ____b. how David finds an answer to his problem all by himself.
    ____c. how David spends four lonely days on an islet.
    ____d. how David meets a friendly innkeeper and stays for the night.

Check your answers with the key on page 68.

This page may be reproduced for classroom use.

Through the Isle of Mull

VOCABULARY CHECK

astonished	beauty	cardboard	cereal	flap	heavens

I. Sentences to Finish

Fill in the blank in each sentence with the correct key word from the box above.

1. The mailman lifted the _____ on his bag and took out two letters for Annie.

2. John was_____to see a tiny ant carrying a large bug on its back.

3. I saw a star fall through the_____and I made a wish.

4. The painting was a thing of _____ , and I looked at it for a long time.

5. There is usually a piece of _____ on the back of a pad of paper.

6. Susan likes to have _____ and eggs for breakfast.

II. Finish the Story

Use the key words from the box above to fill in the spaces in the story so that it makes sense.

I could hardly keep my eyes from closing, as I opened the _____ on the top of the _____ cereal box. I poured the _____ into my bowl. It was still very early and the sun was not up yet. When I finished my breakfast, I went outside and sat in the yard. I was _____ to see such a big orange sun show itself and rise in the _____ .

Its _____ stayed in my mind for a long time.

Check your answers with the key on page 70.

I Meet the Red Fox in Appin

PREPARATION

Key Words

birth	(bərth)	the act of being born or giving life to *Mrs. Gold gave <u>birth</u> to twin girls.*
cozy	(kō ' zē)	warm and comfortable *The thick carpet gave the room a <u>cozy</u> look.*
divide	(də vīd ')	break apart *I wanted to <u>divide</u> the pie, so I cut it in two pieces.* share in *The winners of the contest had to <u>divide</u> the prize money.*
simple	(sim ' pəl)	easy *Fixing the lock was so <u>simple</u>,that Scott did it in five minutes.*
switch	(swich)	change from one thing to another *Chuck decided to <u>switch</u> jobs because he was offered more money.* a button for turning on lights or machines
willing	(wil ' ing)	ready and eager to do something *Lucy was <u>willing</u> to share her lunch with Carla, who had forgotten hers.*

I Meet the Red Fox in Appin

Necessary Words

lad (lad) boy; youth
The lad helped his grandfather do some work around the house.

People

Neil Rob Macrob is a friend of Alan's and the captain of a boat that runs between Torosay on Mull and the mainland of Morven.

Mr. Henderland is a man who preaches religion in Morven.

Places

Appin is in the Highlands of Scotland across the Firth of Lorne from Morven. (See ④ on map, page 67.)

I Meet the Red Fox in Appin

David showed Captain Macrob the silver button Alan had given him.

Preview: 1. Read the name of the story.
2. Look at the picture.
3. Read the sentence under the picture.
4. Read the first three paragraphs of the story.
5. Then answer the following question.

You learned from your preview that
____a. Alan's friends were not very helpful.
____b. the silver button would help David.
____c. there were no boats from Torosay to Morven.
____d. David was in danger after talking to Macrob.

Turn to the Comprehension Check on page 40 for the right answer.

Now read the story.

Read to find out how David will meet the Red Fox.

I Meet the Red Fox in Appin

There is a boat that goes back and forth from Torosay on Mull to the mainland of Morven. I made myself cozy on the ride over. The captain of the boat was Neil Macrob. He was one of Alan Breck Stewart's clan.

When we got to the mainland, I talked to Neil Macrob about Alan. Then I showed him my silver button.

"Ah," said Mr. Macrob, "you are the lad with the silver button. I have been told to keep you safe."

He warned me never to speak the name of Alan Breck out loud to anyone. Then he gave me simple directions, and I was on my way.

Early the next day I met a small quiet man who was reading a book as he walked along. His name was Mr. Henderland, and he tried to divide his time between reading and talking to me. As we talked, I discovered that he knew of Mr. Campbell, the minister from the land of my birth.

I was careful not to speak of Alan, but Henderland talked of him. He spoke ill of Alan. But he did say that there were others that respected Alan greatly. He also said he feared for the life of Colin Roy Campbell, the Red Fox.

The following day, Mr. Henderland found a man with a boat who was willing to take me to Appin with him. From the boat, I could see the red coats of the English soldiers who were coming into Appin. They were coming with the Red Fox to make Alan's people leave their homes.

Soon I set foot on land. It was a black day and the sky was thick with clouds. I sat down to eat some bread. I began to wonder why I was so willing to join a group of outlaws and Alan Breck. Why would I want to switch the simple good ways I had known since my birth for that kind of life? I was feeling cozy among the trees, when I heard the sound of men and horses coming through the woods.

There were four men, and I stopped them for directions. The man in the lead had bright red hair. After talking to him for a short time, I knew he was the Red Fox.

All of a sudden a shot was heard from the hills. "Oh, I am dead!" cried the Red Fox.

One of the men caught him before he fell. But it was too late. I could see the killer running away. He was wearing a black coat.

"I see the killer," I cried. Just then, I heard one of the men shouting to the soldiers. He told them to come after me. He said I had stopped them as part of a plan to kill the Red Fox.

I started running up a hill in fear of the soldiers. My heart was pounding.

"Duck in here among the trees," a voice whispered to me. I hardly knew what I was doing, but I did as I was told.

Inside the many rows of trees I found Alan Breck. "Run fast and follow me!" he ordered. And I followed at great speed. Carefully, we went around the mountain and back to the place where we had begun. My head was turning around and my sides hurt from running so fast. We finally dropped like two dead men.

When we both awakened, Alan was ready to go on, but I told him I could not go with him. I said I could not forget how he had killed the Red Fox so coldly. Alan told me he had not done it. He would never do such a thing in his own part of the country. It would bring trouble to his friends and family.

I believed what Alan said. Now he would have to switch his old plan for a new one. We would leave the country as quickly as we could. People would believe we had a part in the killing of the Red Fox. Soon, more soldiers would be searching for us.

Alan and I would not divide up. We would stay together and make our way. Our journey would be hard and the days would be long.

I Meet the Red Fox in Appin

COMPREHENSION CHECK

Choose the best answer.

1. Mr. Henderland
   ____a. never heard of Mr. Campbell the minister.
   ____b. liked Alan Breck Stewart's ways.
   ____c. helped David reach the land of Appin.
   ____d. never spoke about the Red Fox.

2. The English soldiers and the Red Fox
   ____a. were going to help the people of Appin.
   ____b. were coming to Appin to make the people give up their lands.
   ____c. were bringing good news to Alan Breck Stewart.
   ____d. were coming to take David back to Essendean and Mr. Campbell.

3. The Red Fox
   ____a. had a bright red coat.
   ____b. had a red horse.
   ____c. had a red fox.
   ____d. had bright red hair.

4. While David was talking with the Red Fox,
   ____a. Alan Breck got away.
   ____b. the soldiers took David.
   ____c. the Red Fox was killed.
   ____d. Mr. Henderland was killed.

5. The soldiers were looking for David because
   ____a. he said he saw who killed the Red Fox.
   ____b. they knew he was a friend of Mr. Henderland.
   ____c. someone thought he had been part of the plan to kill the Red Fox.
   ____d. they thought he took some money from a man along the way.

6. Alan Breck Stewart
   ____a. was a smart man who planned his way well.
   ____b. was not very helpful to David.
   ____c. was the killer of the Red Fox.
   ____d. was ready to give himself to the soldiers.

7. From what Mr. Henderland said, we know that
   ____a. some people liked Alan and what he did, and others did not.
   ____b. Alan was loved by everyone in Scotland at this time.
   ____c. the Red Fox was the safest man in Appin.
   ____d. David told him that he knew Alan Breck.

8. By the end of the story,
   ____a. the soldiers have found David and Alan.
   ____b. Alan and David have joined together again.
   ____c. the Red Fox is still alive in Scotland.
   ____d. Alan and David are going different ways.

9. Another name for this story could be
   ____a. "I Get a Silver Button."
   ____b. "My Adventures In Appin."
   ____c. "Meeting Mr. Henderland."
   ____d. "Taking a Boat Ride."

10. This story is mainly about
   ____a. how the soldiers plan to find David and Alan in the woods of Appin.
   ____b. how the Red Fox travels through Appin with a group of soldiers.
   ____c. how David journeys to Appin and meets Alan during a time of trouble.
   ____d. how meeting a man like Mr. Henderland can change a young man's life.

Check your answers with the key of page 68.

I Meet the Red Fox in Appin

VOCABULARY CHECK

birth	cozy	divide	simple	switch	willing

I. Sentences to Finish

Fill in the blank in each sentence with the correct key word from the box above.

1. The young parents were excited about the _____ of their first child.

2. I was _____ to get a job to pay for my schooling.

3. Since Mary had no lunch, I decided to _____ my sandwich in half and share it with her.

4. Mrs. Jones said she would _____ my red shirt for a blue one.

5. The light and heat from the fire made the room feel _____ .

6. The math problem was so _____ ,that I finished it quickly and went on to the next one.

II. Making Sense of Sentences

Do the statements below make sense? Place a check next to the correct answer.

1. A person's <u>birth</u> is the end of his or her life.

   _____True _____False

2. Something <u>simple</u> to understand is hard to understand.

   _____True _____False

3. A <u>cozy</u> house is warm and comfortable.

   _____True _____False

4. If you <u>divide</u> something, you put it together.

   _____True _____False

5. In order to <u>switch</u> books, you must change one for another.

   _____True _____False

6. If you are <u>willing</u> to do something, you are ready or eager.

   _____True _____False

Check your answers with the key on page 70.

Alan and I Escape in the Heather

PREPARATION

Key Words

bedroom	(bed ′ rüm)	a room used for sleeping *Go into the bedroom and wake him up.*
brick	(brik)	hard block used to make walls or walks *We walked up the brick path to the house.*
clothing	(klō ′ ᵵHing)	coverings for the body *We should wear heavy clothing when it is cold.*
lovely	(luv ′ lē)	beautiful; happy; nice *It is a lovely day to ride.*
note	(nōt)	a few words put on paper to help one remember *This note will tell you the things you should buy at the store.*
twice	(twīs)	two times *I called her twice before she answered.*

Alan and I Escape in the Heather

Necessary Words

heather   (heᴛн ′ ər)   a low evergreen bush of the heath family with small purple or pink flowers that covers much of the open land in Scotland and England
      The heather was a good place to hide.

jail   (jāl)   a place where people who are being punished by the law are kept
      The man was sent to jail for stealing a car.

People

James Stewart   is the half-brother of the chief of Alan's clan.

John Breck Maccoll   is a friend of Alan's in Appin.

Alan and I Escape in the Heather

It was dark when David and Alan came upon the home of James Stewart, one of Alan's clan. There were many people walking around the house.

Preview: 1.   Read the name of the story.
2.   Look at the picture.
3.   Read the sentences under the picture.
4.   Read the first two paragraphs of the story.
5.   Then answer the following question.

You learned from your preview that
_____a. David had just gotten back to the house of Shaws.
_____b. the chief of Alan's clan was in Appin, Scotland.
_____c. something strange was going on at James Stewart's house.
_____d. Alan came upon James Stewart's house alone.

Turn to the Comprehension Check on page 46 for the right answer.

Now read the story.

Read to find out what was happening at James Stewart's house and why.

Alan and I Escape in the Heather

Night fell as we walked to the home of Alan's cousin, James Stewart. James was a half brother to the chief of Alan's clan. He spoke for the chief, since the chief had to be sent to France for safekeeping.

At half past ten on the clock, we came to the top of a hill that looked over James's brick house. Light streamed through all the windows. All the doors were wide open and many people walked around the house. They all held lights.

"James must have lost his mind," said Alan. "If we were soldiers, they would all be in real trouble right now."

Alan whistled three times in a certain way to let them know who we were. First they stopped. Then they went back to searching out and carrying away guns and swords. They were burying them down the road.

When we came down the hill, we were met by James. He was a good-looking man of about fifty years. James and Alan spoke about the killing of the Red Fox. There was real danger to everyone in their clan.

James and I sat in the kitchen with his family. Alan went into the bedroom to change into other French clothing. Mrs. Stewart was a lovely woman, but she sat in the corner of the room weeping. She knew what terrible things might happen to them.

I was glad when Alan came back from the bedroom. The sorrow in the room was too much for me. It was my turn to get a change of clothes.

By the time I came back, Alan had told our story. It was understood that we would leave together right away. Each of us was given a sword and a gun. We were also given food and drink. We had little money left by now, and James had none to give.

"You cannot stay here and wait for money," said James. "They will come looking for you. I have a family to think about. And it would be a terrible thing for our friends if I were to hang."

James said he would have to think of himself and his family first. Since we were wanted by the law anyway, he, too, would have to name us in the killing. Neither James nor Alan would ever tell who really killed the Red Fox, even though they both knew.

We left to hide in the heather. We would send word to James later, and he would send money. Sometimes we walked and other times we ran. Twice along the way we stopped at houses so Alan could tell people the news.

The days were long and the nights even longer. On a clear day, we could see the soldiers in the distance. Then we ran a little faster and a little farther to make our escape.

It was the beginning of July. We reached the place we were going in the dark of the morning. We slept in a cave, making our beds from heather bushes. We lit a small fire and cooked the fish we caught in a small stream. There was much time, so Alan taught me how to use my sword.

The first morning, Alan said we had to get word to James. Alan had a friend nearby who could get our words to him. Since this man could not read, a note would be of little use, so Alan made a sign to put in the man's window. The man would understand our danger and know where we were hiding.

John Breck Maccoll understood Alan's sign and came to us. Alan gave him a note to take to James. Three days later, John returned with a note from Mrs. Stewart. James was in jail.

Mrs. Stewart sent us a small amount of money and a paper that told about Alan and me. Anyone who found us would be paid well. The paper said Alan was wearing French clothing. But my new clothes did not match what it said about me.

We read the paper twice. We could not believe how much money was being offered for us. Then we left the cave and went on to a safer place.

Alan and I Escape in the Heather

COMPREHENSION CHECK

Choose the best answer.

1. James Stewart
    _____a. was in France for safekeeping.
    _____b. was a friend of the Red Fox.
    _____c. was an important man in Alan's clan.
    _____d. was not afraid of what might happen to him.

2. The people at James Stewart's house were
    _____a. taking guns away and hiding them.
    _____b. building a garage for Alan to hide in.
    _____c. bringing guns for James to use.
    _____d. acting as soldiers for the king.

3. It was believed that
    _____a. King George had turned away from the Red Fox.
    _____b. one of the soldiers had killed the Red Fox by accident.
    _____c. Uncle Ebenezer had killed the Red Fox.
    _____d. Alan's clan was to blame for the killing of the Red Fox.

4. In the cave, Alan and David made beds from
    _____a. feathers.
    _____b. rocks.
    _____c. heather.
    _____d. grass.

5. Alan made a sign for John Maccoll because
    _____a. John could not see.
    _____b. John could not read.
    _____c. Alan could not write.
    _____d. David could not walk.

6. While Alan and David were making their way to the cave,
    _____a. James Stewart was put in jail for the killing of the Red Fox.
    _____b. John Maccoll told the soldiers where they were hiding.
    _____c. James Stewart moved his family and got away safely.
    _____d. Mrs. Stewart was put in jail for the killing of the Red Fox.

7. Which **two** of the following were in the paper that told about Alan and David?
    _____a. Alan was wearing French clothing.
    _____b. There was a good bit of money being offered to anyone who found the two.
    _____c. An idea about how David had changed his clothing.
    _____d. They had helped James Stewart bury the guns he was keeping.

8. If David and Alan wanted to get away,
    _____a. they should have stayed in one place.
    _____b. they would have given up to the soldiers.
    _____c. they had to keep moving and hiding.
    _____d. they had to buy a car very soon.

9. Another name for this story could be
    _____a. ''Running From the King's Soldiers.''
    _____b. ''Playing in the Fields.''
    _____c. ''Lost in a Cave.''
    _____d. ''Learning How to Use a Sword.''

10. This story is mainly about
    _____d. how David uses his sword at the cave.
    _____b. how James Stewart makes himself safe.
    _____c. how David and Alan get help from Alan's friends while making their way through Appin.
    _____d. how John Maccoll learns to read when he has to understand Alan's note.

Check your answers with the key on page 68.

This page may be reproduced for classroom use.

Alan and I Escape in the Heather

VOCABULARY CHECK

bedroom	brick	clothing	lovely	note	twice

I. Sentences to Finish

Fill in the blank in each sentence with the correct key word from the box above.

1. My brother and I have bunk beds in our _____ .

2. I left a _____ to let my mother know I had gone to the store.

3. Judy has a _____ smile and a friendly way.

4. Andrew built a _____ wall around his house.

5. I had to look _____ before I was sure it was my old friend Jim.

6. His _____ was worn and dirty after his long journey through the woods.

II. Words and their Meanings

Put a check next to the word that means the same thing as the underlined word or words in each sentence.

1. I changed my <u>coverings for the body</u> after my run.
   ____ a. note   ____ c. brick
   ____ b. clothing   ____ d. bedroom

2. I like to rest and read in my <u>room used for sleeping</u>.
   ____ a. brick   ____ c. bedroom
   ____ b. living room   ____ d. note

3. The sky was clear and it was a <u>beautiful</u> day.
   ____ a. lovely   ____ c. terrible
   ____ b. simple   ____ d. stray

4. I wrote a <u>few words on paper</u> and slipped it under Kim's door.
   ____ a. brick   ____ c. bedroom
   ____ b. pitcher   ____ d. note

5. The house was made of red <u>hard block</u>.
   ____ a. wood   ____ c. windows
   ____ b. brick   ____ d. bedrooms

6. I read the book <u>two times</u> because I enjoyed it so much.
   ____ a. lovely   ____ c. twice
   ____ b. once   ____ d. rapidly

Check your answers with the key on page 71.

This page may be reproduced for classroom use.

Cluny's Cage

PREPARATION

Key Words

coward	(kou ′ ərd)	someone who has no courage or who is afraid *Eric knew he had to jump off the diving board or be called a <u>coward</u> by the other boys.*
faithful	(fāth ′ fəl)	believing in or trusting someone *The blind man's <u>faithful</u> dog led him safely across the street.*
gaze	(gāz)	stare *Ann stopped to <u>gaze</u> at the diamond rings in the store window.*
impossible	(im pos ′ ə bəl)	not able to happen *People once thought it was <u>impossible</u> for a man to walk on the moon.*
inquire	(in kwīr ′)	ask about *Josh called to <u>inquire</u> about the time of the meeting.*
sore	(sôr, sōr)	a place on the body where the skin has been hurt *Pepe had a big <u>sore</u> on his leg from the bee sting.* hurting *After calling my dog Ben for an hour, my throat was <u>sore</u>.*

Cluny's Cage

People

Cluny Macpherson   is the chief of the clan Vourich.

Places

Ben Alder   is a mountain in the Highlands. (See ⑤ on map, page 67.)

Loch Rannoch   is a lake in the Highlands. (See ⑥ on map, page 67.)

Cluny's Cage

Alan and David raced toward the wild, desert mountain called Ben Alder.

Preview:
1. Read the name of the story.
2. Look at the picture.
3. Read the sentence under the picture.
4. Read the first three paragraphs of the story.
5. Then answer the following question.

You learned from your preview that
____a. Alan had fallen asleep while on watch.
____b. David and Alan were in some kind of danger.
____c. it was a cool day in the heather.
____d. the two men did not have far to go.

Turn to the Comprehension Check on page 52 for the right answer.

Now read the story.

Read to find out if Alan and David will be able to continue their journey.

Cluny's Cage

After many hours of hard travelling, we came to the end of a group of mountains. In front of us was a low desert land which we now had to cross. It was early morning and we sat down for a time to make our plans. Alan knew every part of the Highlands. We would go east.

We crawled on our bellies from heather bush to heather bush. The sun was hot and I was careful not to gaze up at it. Our bottle of drink was gone, and the long road ahead seemed like an impossible one to complete.

By noon it was even hotter, and my hands and knees were sore. We stopped to lie down in a thick heather bush. Alan took the first watch. When it was my turn, I had trouble keeping my sore eyes open. I must have closed them for too long. When I awakened, I gazed at a terrible sight.

Quickly, I woke up Alan. Ahead of us was a body of soldiers riding in our direction.

"What will we do?" I inquired of Alan.

"We'll have to race to that mountain over there like rabbits," answered Alan Breck Stewart. "It's a wild, desert mountain called Ben Alder."

I put my trust in my faithful friend. It was no time to be a coward. We crawled from heather bush to heather bush. Finding a safe place seemed almost impossible.

We were running down a heathery path, when there was a noise. Suddenly, we were on our backs with knives at our throats. Our guns and swords were taken. It was terrible, but I was so tired that I was glad to lie still.

Alan was no coward. He began to inquire as to who these men were. They were faithful followers of the clan called Vourich, led by Cluny Macpherson.

Alan knew of him. Cluny had been in charge of a great fight against the English king six years before, and he, too, was a wanted man. There was a price on his head, just as there was on ours.

One of the men left us for a time. When he came back, he said Cluny would see us. We were taken to a strange place called *Cluny's Cage*. It was on top of that awful mountain Ben Alder. It was one of many of Cluny's hiding places. Here we were fed and hidden for several days.

Cluny's Cage was strange, indeed. And Cluny was a man quite set in his ways. Nothing in his place could be moved. Friends came to visit, but Cluny never left while we were there.

Most of the time at Cluny's, I was sick in bed. One night, Cluny and Alan got into a card game. Alan came and asked me for my money while I was half asleep. He lost all his money and mine. I was very angry with him when I woke up and found out what he had done.

Before we left, Cluny gave me back the money he had won from Alan. Then he shook my hand, and Alan and I were on our way again. Cluny's people would take us to a safe place past Loch Rannoch.

We were taken away under cloud of night. For many miles we did not speak. I kept thinking of how Alan had been so sneaky about losing my money. And my anger grew.

I was just getting over my sickness, and I was rained on day and night. After a few days in the heather, I could hardly walk. Finally, all my angry words flew from my mouth, and Alan and I fought with words.

Then I was too weak to be angry, and I was sorry. My friend Alan came to my side. He carried me along the path.

"We must find a house for you to rest," said Alan. And after all I had said, I wondered why he still cared anything about me.

Cluny's Cage

COMPREHENSION CHECK

Choose the best answer.

1.   Cluny Macpherson
_____a. was free to wander in the Highlands.
_____b. was a friend to the English king.
_____c. was wanted by the law and had to hide all the time.
_____d. was not willing to hide David and Alan at his place.

2.   Cluny's Cage
_____a. was under the Firth of Forth.
_____b. was on top of a mountain called Ben Alder.
_____c. was in the country of England.
_____d. was on a beautiful island.

3.   David was angry at Alan because
_____a. Alan had run off in the night with Cluny Macpherson.
_____b. Alan would not stop to rest.
_____c. Alan had fallen asleep on watch.
_____d. Alan had been sneaky about getting David's money.

4.   During most of this story
_____a. David is very sick.
_____b. Alan is ready to give up.
_____c. David is leading the way.
_____d. Alan is very sick.

5.   Alan
_____a. was always right in everything he did at Cluny's Cage.
_____b. did not get along with Cluny Macpherson.
_____c. showed a poor side of himself at Cluny's Cage.
_____d. wanted to leave David when David got sick.

6.   David
_____a. looked to Alan to help and lead him.
_____b. did not feel sorry about what he said to Alan.
_____c. was not liked by Cluny Macpherson.
_____d. would have been able to travel on his own.

7.   Most of the time, Alan Breck Stewart
_____a. made the wrong choices.
_____b. did the right things and took good care of David.
_____c. did not know his way through the Highlands.
_____d. was not sure of himself.

8.   At the end of the story, David and Alan
_____a. are caught by the soldiers.
_____b. do not like each other anymore.
_____c. are both feeling sick.
_____d. are friends again.

9.   Another name for this story could be
_____a. "Saved By Cluny's Clan."
_____b. "Escape on a Boat."
_____c. "There Is No Safe Place."
_____d. "An Island Hiding Place."

10.   This story is mainly about
_____a. the way David and Alan fight with the soldiers in the heather.
_____b. the time David and Alan spend with Cluny and his people.
_____c. the way David feels about Cluny Macpherson.
_____d. the place where David sees the soldiers.

Check your answers with the key on page 68.

Cluny's Cage

VOCABULARY CHECK

coward	faithful	gaze	impossible	inquire	sore

I. Sentences to Finish

Fill in the blank in each sentence with the correct key word from the box above.

1. I telephoned the movie to _____ about the time of the first show.

2. The soldier thought himself a _____ when he turned and ran from the fighting.

3. After John ran two miles, his feet were very _____ .

4. My _____ dog led me through the woods to the safety of my camp.

5. On a clear night I like to _____ at the stars.

6. Blind skiers have shown that it is not _____ for people without sight to ski and have fun.

II. Finish the Story

Use the key words from the box above to fill in the spaces in the story so that it makes sense.

David fixed his _____ on the soldiers that were riding through the heather. He quickly woke up Alan to _____ about what to do.

David did not want to seem like a _____ , so he followed his _____ friend Alan. After crawling through the heather for hours, David was tired and his hands and feet were _____ . He began to think it was _____ for them to get away.

Check your answers with the key on page 71.

My Journey to Mr. Rankeillor

PREPARATION

Key Words

complain	(kəm plān´)	say that something is wrong *The man will complain if the ball hits the window.*
content	(kon tent´)	happy; not wanting anything else *The boy was content to sit and play in the sand.*
greedy	(grē´ dē)	wanting to eat and drink a lot in a hurry *Because he was so hungry, he was a greedy animal when we fed him.* having a strong wish to own things *The greedy man could never get enough money to make him happy, even though he had much more than he needed.*
message	(mes´ ij)	words or ideas given by one person to another *The woman called on the telephone and left a message for you.*
recognize	(rek´ əg nīz)	to know a person or place because you have seen it before *The baby began to recognize her grandmother.*
route	(rüt, rout)	the road to take from one place to another *The bus takes the same route to school each day.*

My Journey to Mr. Rankeillor

People

**Mr. and
  Mrs. Maclaren**
are a husband and wife that belong to the Maclaren family of Balquhidder. They are friends of Alan's clan.

Places

Balquhidder
is a place in the Highlands. (See ⑦ on map, page 67.)

Stirling
is a town on the River Forth where there is a bridge to cross the river. (See ⑧ on map, page 67.)

Limekilns
is a town across the River Forth from Queensferry. (See ⑨ on map, page 67.)

Queensferry
is the town that lies on the River Forth near the Queen's Ferry, where David was kidnapped on the Covenant in an earlier part of the book. (See ⑩ on map, page 67.)

Things

bagpipe
(bag ′ pīp)
is a musical instrument made up of a leather bag and five wooden pipes. The player blows air into the bag through one pipe. Then the air is forced out of the bag through four pipes that make the sounds.

My Journey to Mr. Rankeillor

In Queensferry, David came upon Mr. Rankeillor, the lawyer, quite by accident.

Preview:
1. Read the name of the story.
2. Look at the picture.
3. Read the sentence under the picture.
4. Read the first three paragraphs of the story.
5. Then answer the following question.

You learned from your preview that
____a. David and Alan had come to a safe place.
____b. Alan would not take any chances for David.
____c. David and Alan were treated badly by the Maclarens.
____d. David would never get to Queensferry.

Turn to the Comprehension Check on page 58 for the right answer.

Now read the story.

Read to find out where Alan and David will go next.

My Journey to Mr. Rankeillor

At the door of the first house we came upon, Alan knocked. This was not the safest thing to do in this part of the country called Balquhidder.

The house was full of Maclarens, which came to the same thing as Stewarts. And since Alan Breck was a Stewart, and well-known in these parts, we were most welcome.

I was so sick that I was content to go right to bed. They called for a doctor. Though I was not one to be greedy, I enjoyed the care I received those days.

I was a strong young man and was able to get out of bed in a week. Within a month, I was ready to follow a new route to safety.

All this time, Alan had been hiding in the thick of the woods by day. At night, if all was well, he came to visit me. I was pleased by his visits, but I told him he was taking a big chance.

Mrs. Maclaren was so pleased at having Alan in her house, she could not do enough for him. Mr. Maclaren played his bagpipe for us. This turned the dark long nights into fun and we all had a merry time.

I was finally able to leave and take to the road. Alan and I could not complain about the weather. It was August. Summer was almost over and the warm signs of autumn were all around.

We were almost out of money by now, and if we did not reach Mr. Rankeillor the lawyer, soon, we would surely go hungry. Our first night was spent at a Maclaren's house in a nearby village. After that, we slept in heather bushes on the hillsides. Sleep was always a welcome thing.

After two days, we had passed the Highland Line and we came upon the river called the Forth. We had to cross the river to get to Queensferry and Mr. Rankeillor. There was no other route. But there were soldiers on the Stirling Bridge, and we had no boat.

Alan had a plan and we walked all night until we reached the town of Limekilns that looked over the river to Queensferry. We entered an inn and a lovely young woman brought us bread and cheese.

Alan was not content to let help pass us by. He complained so much about my illness, that the young lady offered to help us cross the river. She seemed afraid at first, until I said I was bringing a message to Mr. Rankeillor the lawyer. She knew of him and wanted to help.

The young woman left her house at night and took a neighbor's boat. She came by herself to take us across the river to Queensferry. We waved a sad good-bye upon reaching the other side.

The next day, Alan and I agreed that he should go his own way until darkness. I found my way to Mr. Rankeillor's house quite by accident. The lawyer was just walking out his front door when I stopped to ask him directions.

Mr. Rankeillor was quite surprised that I was searching for him. He could not have recognized me as the son of Alexander Balfour in such worn, torn and dirty clothes.

We entered his house and he began to ask me many questions about my background. He listened with great interest as I told my story. I began with Uncle Ebenezer's wrongdoings and went on with my adventures in the Highlands.

Mr. Rankeillor asked only one thing of me. If someone in my story went against the law, he should not be called by his right name. So Alan Breck Stewart became Mr. Thompson for the rest of my story.

The ship Covenant was lost on June the 27th, and it was now August the 24th. And my friend Mr. Campbell the minister had come to Mr. Rankeillor, on the very day of the shipwreck, looking for me.

When I finished my tale, I could see that Mr. Rankeillor received my message. He asked me to stay for dinner. And he gave me his son's clothes to put on. When I looked in the mirror, I could hardly recognize myself. David Balfour had come to life again.

My Journey to Mr. Rankeillor

COMPREHENSION CHECK

Choose the best answer.

1. Alan Breck
    _____a. had to hide in the woods near the Maclaren's house.
    _____b. was able to run through Balquhidder freely.
    _____c. stayed at the Maclaren's all day with David.
    _____d. was hated by the Maclarens of Balquhidder.

2. At the Stirling Bridge,
    _____a. David and Alan crossed the River Forth.
    _____b. David and Alan returned to Cluny's Cage.
    _____c. David and Alan found soldiers in their way.
    _____d. David and Alan said good-bye to each other.

3. Alan
    _____a. could not think of a plan.
    _____b. said nothing to the young lady in the inn.
    _____c. really thought David was still very sick.
    _____d. had a very good plan.

4. Alan and David got to Queensferry
    _____a. by taking a boat away from a young lady by force.
    _____b. when a young lady took them across the Forth by boat.
    _____c. by calling to Mr. Rankeillor across the River Forth.
    _____d. when the Covenant stopped and picked them up.

5. After the wreck of the Covenant, David had been missing for about
    _____a. two years.
    _____b. two weeks.
    _____c. two months.
    _____d. two days.

6. Mr. Campbell the minister
    _____a. did not think about David once the boy left Essendean.
    _____b. went to see Alan Breck about David.
    _____c. was probably very worried because he had not heard from David.
    _____d. was not really a friend to David.

7. Mr. Thompson
    _____a. was a friend of Mr. Rankeillor.
    _____b. was no one David knew.
    _____c. was someone who lived in Queensferry.
    _____d. was really Alan Breck Stewart.

8. Mr. Rankeillor
    _____a. treated David Balfour with kindness.
    _____b. sent David Balfour away when he saw him.
    _____c. asked David to tell him Alan's real name.
    _____d. called David's Uncle Ebenezer right away.

9. Another name for this story could be
    _____a. ''I Leave Queensferry.''
    _____b. ''I Tell Mr. Rankeillor My Story.''
    _____c. ''I Become a Sailor.''
    _____d. ''I Meet a Young Lady and Marry.''

10. This story is mainly about
    _____a. how David gets to Queensferry and talks to Mr. Rankeillor.
    _____b. how Alan Breck goes to Mr. Rankeillor with David's story.
    _____c. how Uncle Ebenezer searches for David.
    _____d. how David returns to the Highlands.

Check your answers with the key of page 68.

My Journey to Mr. Rankeillor

VOCABULARY CHECK

complain	content	greedy	message	recognize	route

I. Sentences to Finish

Fill in the blank in each sentence with the correct key word from the box above.

1. After being away for so many years, Paul was sure he would still _____ the people from his old home town.

2. Everyone in the store began to _____ about the poor way they were being helped.

3. Sally's _____ said that she would be going to the library after school.

4. The baby was _____ to drink his bottle of warm milk.

5. John was in a hurry, so he took the shortest _____ home.

6. The cat was _____ about his food and would not share any of his meals with the dog.

II. Crossword Puzzle

Fill in the puzzle with the key words from the box above. Use the meanings below to help you choose the right word.

Across

2. having a great want to own things

4. say that something is wrong

6. not wanting anything else

Down

1. words or ideas given to one person by another

3. to know a person or place because you have seen it before

5. the road to take from one place to another

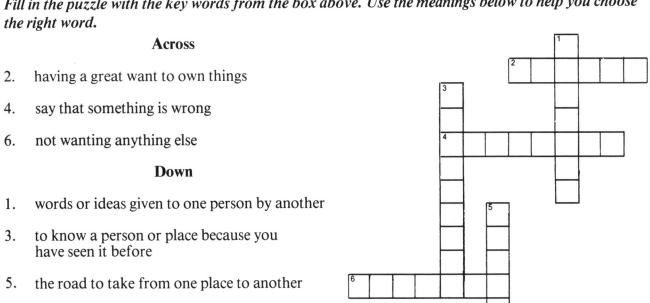

Check your answers with the key on page 71.

This page may be reproduced for classroom use.

I Come to Own What Is Mine

PREPARATION

Key Words

average   (av ′ ər ij)   usual; common
> *You must do better than average work to be listed on the honor roll.*

butcher   (búch ′ ər)   a man who sells meat
> *We bought our hot dogs at the butcher shop.*

copy   (kop ′ ē)   something made to look just like something else
> *This list is a copy of the list I have at home.*

loft   (lôft)   the top floor in a barn
> *We store hay for the winter in the loft of the barn.*

the space just below the roof of a house
> *My mother keeps old furniture in the loft.*

pitch   (pich)   throw or toss
> *It is your turn to pitch the ball.*

selfish   (sel ′ fish)   not caring for others
> *He was a selfish man who thought only of himself.*

I Come to Own What Is Mine

Necessary Words

admire (ad mīr ') look on someone or something with delight
Each time we were at the art show, I would <u>admire</u> the same painting.

kidnap (kid ' nap) carry off a person or child by force
Captain Hoseason said he would <u>kidnap</u> David and keep the boy on his ship.

tale (tāl) story
I listened carefully while the sailor told me an exciting <u>tale</u> of the sea.

I Come to Own What Is Mine

At the house of Shaws, David and Mr. Rankeillor hid while Alan carried out their plan.

Preview:
1. Read the name of the story.
2. Look at the picture.
3. Read the sentence under the picture.
4. Read the first three paragraphs of the story.
5. Then answer the following question.

You learned from your preview that
____a. Alexander and Ebenezer were very poor.
____b. David's mother had a part in the story of the Shaws.
____c. Uncle Ebenezer had never been selfish before he got old.
____d. David was not a Balfour of Shaws.

Turn to the Comprehension Check on page 64 for the right answer.

Now read the story.

Read to find out the truth about the house of Shaws.

I Come to Own What Is Mine

Mr. Rankeillor was sure that I would want to know the story about my father and my Uncle Ebenezer. He asked me to sit down and he began.

"This is not your average tale," said the lawyer. Then he told me that my father and my uncle were brought up quite well. Uncle Ebenezer had been better looking and more admired than my father. Both men had fallen in love with the same young lady. That lady was my mother.

"Uncle Ebenezer had always been selfish and spoiled, so he was sure he had won the lady's hand. But that was not true. The lady loved your father," said Mr. Rankeillor.

"Ebenezer made himself sick over this thing and your father felt sorry. Your father gave in to one thing and then another. Finally, there was a kind of bargain. Your father would marry the lady and your uncle would have all that belonged to the Shaws.

"When your father was suddenly gone, people thought Ebenezer had killed him. Because of this, no one would speak to your uncle. Your parents lived and died poor, but happy. Ebenezer grew old and more selfish."

Mr. Rankeillor said that whatever was the Shaws would belong to me. But he thought it best that Uncle Ebenezer keep the house, where he had lived all his life. I would receive an average amount of money that was really mine.

Mr. Rankeillor and I thought of a way to handle my Uncle Ebenezer. Alan would help carry out the plan.

The next day, Mr. Rankeillor, his clerk, Alan and I headed for the house of Shaws. We all hid behind a corner of the house while Alan went up to the door and knocked.

My uncle called down to Alan from the loft. Then he came to the door. Alan told him that he knew I had been kidnapped. Alan said he was a friend of Captain Hoseason, and knew all about the way my uncle had gotten rid of me.

At first my uncle said none of it was true. But Alan cut through his words like a butcher cuts through meat. Finally, my uncle told the truth. He'd given Captain Hoseason money to sell me as a slave.

If this story had fallen on a stranger's ears, he would have thought my uncle a terrible butcher of a man.

When the talking was over, Mr. Rankeillor stepped forward. He said he had heard every word. Uncle Ebenezer stared at us like a man turned to stone.

Mr. Rankeillor pitched Ebenezer into the house. They talked for a time. It was agreed that I would get two thirds of the Shaws' money each year. My uncle signed one copy of this paper and I signed another.

That night, we all had drinks and dinner. Mr. Rankeillor and the clerk slept in the loft. I sat in front of the fire for many hours. I thought of all that had happened.

The next day, we all headed for town. Mr. Rankeillor told me about a lawyer who could help Alan. Then he told me what to do and where to go so that Alan could be on his way. I was happy to offer my money and take any chance to get Alan out of the country.

I spoke to Mr. Rankeillor about James Stewart, who had been jailed for the killing of the Red Fox. It would be dangerous, but I wanted to tell the law that he did not do the killing. Mr. Rankeillor gave me a letter to take with me, and wished me the best.

Alan and I knew we were coming to the time when we must part. Neither of us could speak. Alan would hide until his trip was set. We would meet one time a day to talk.

Alan and I had a special kind of friendship. We had been through much together. Our parting came at a place called Rest-and-be-Thankful. We each said a simple goodbye.

I walked through the busy streets of Edinburgh. There was much to see and hear. But all I could think about was Rest-and-be-Thankful. And how thankful I was to have known Alan Breck Stewart.

I Come to Own What Is Mine

COMPREHENSION CHECK

Choose the best answer.

1. David's father, Alexander
   _____a. would not give in to his brother, Ebenezer.
   _____b. was a spoiled and selfish man.
   _____c. had given up all that was his to marry David's mother.
   _____d. was killed by his brother when he was young.

2. Mr. Rankeillor
   _____a. told David to take the house of Shaws from his uncle.
   _____b. did not want David to go to the house of Shaws.
   _____c. said David should get the money that was his, but not the house.
   _____d. did not want David to know the truth about Ebenezer and Alexander.

3. Alan Breck Stewart
   _____a. would not help David carry out his plan.
   _____b. warned Uncle Ebenezer about David's plan.
   _____c. was not good at tricking people.
   _____d. tricked David's uncle into telling the truth.

4. Uncle Ebenezer
   _____a. was forced to give David what belonged to him.
   _____b. was happy to give David what was his share of things.
   _____c. was glad to see David at the house of Shaws.
   _____d. was not surprised when Mr. Rankeillor came out from hiding.

5. David Balfour
   _____a. did not think too much about his life and plans.
   _____b. would have a whole new life ahead of him.
   _____c. was not pleased with what he got from his uncle.
   _____d. would not help Alan Breck leave the country.

6. Telling the truth and doing the right thing
   _____a. did not mean much to David Balfour.
   _____b. were important to Ebenezer Balfour.
   _____c. did not help David Balfour in his life.
   _____d. were very important to David Balfour.

7. By the end of the story, David and Alan
   _____a. had helped each other very much.
   _____b. were sorry to have ever met.
   _____c. were tired of being together.
   _____d. had to go back to the Highlands.

8. Alan Breck and David
   _____a. were never very good friends.
   _____b. would never have to say good-bye.
   _____c. were both proud and strong.
   _____d. would not be special to one another.

9. Another name for this story could be
   _____a. "A Happy Time and a Sad One."
   _____b. "Uncle Ebenezer Finds Friends."
   _____c. "James Stewart Is Free."
   _____d. "Mr. Campbell Goes to Queensferry."

10. This story is mainly about
    _____a. how Mr. Rankeillor finds Alan Breck Stewart.
    _____b. how Uncle Ebenezer welcomes David back to the house of Shaws.
    _____c. how the people of Cramond feel sorry for Ebenezer.
    _____d. how David and Alan join together in one more plan before saying good-bye.

Check your answers with the key of page 68.

I Come to Own What Is Mine

VOCABULARY CHECK

average	butcher	copy	loft	pitch	selfish

I. Sentences to Finish

Fill in the blank in each sentence with the correct key word from the box above.

1. The _____ age at which children begin school is five years.

2. The music teacher made a _____ of the new song for each child in her class.

3. My uncle likes to _____ horseshoes at a short pole in his yard.

4. The _____ cut the meat and wrapped it in special paper.

5. John showed how _____ he was when he went home without helping his friend clean up the toys.

6. We used to hide behind the hay in the _____ of my grandfather's barn.

II. Making Sense of Sentences

Do the statements below make sense? Place a check next to the correct answer.

1. If something is <u>average</u>, it is very different.

    _____True _____False

2. A <u>selfish</u> person would think of others first.

    _____True _____False

3. A <u>copy</u> of something looks just like it.

    _____True _____False

4. When you <u>pitch</u> a stone, you use your arm.

    _____True _____False

5. A deep hole under a barn is a <u>loft</u>.

    _____True _____False

6. A <u>butcher</u> plants corn and wheat.

    _____True _____False

Check your answers with the key on page 72.

This page may be reproduced for classroom use.

NOTES

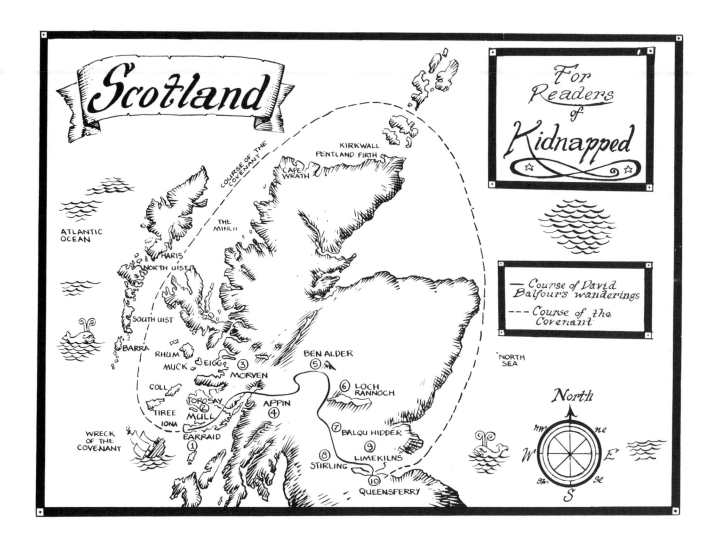

(1.) **EARRAID**

(2.) **MULL and TOROSAY**

(3.) **MORVEN**

(4.) **APPIN**

(5.) **BEN ALDER**

(6.) **LOCH RANNOCH**

(7.) **BALQUHIDDER**

(8.) **STIRLING**

(9.) **LIMEKILNS**

(10.) **QUEENSFERRY**

COMPREHENSION CHECK ANSWER KEY
Lessons CTR C-21 to CTR C-30

LESSON NUMBER	QUESTION NUMBER										PAGE NUMBER
	1	2	3	4	5	6	7	8	9	10	
CTR C-21	b	c	(a)	d	b	(c)	b	d	△d	□b	10
CTR C-22	c	(c)	a	a	a,b	c	d	d	△b	□a	16
CTR C-23	b	c	a	d	a	d	(b)	(d)	△b	□d	22
CTR C-24	b	d	b	d	a	c	(a)	b	△c	□b	28
CTR C-25	a	(c)	c	d	b	a	a,d	d	△b	□c	34
CTR C-26	c	b	d	c	c	(a)	a	b	△b	□c	40
CTR C-27	c	a	d	c	b	a	a,b	(c)	△a	□c	46
CTR C-28	c	b	d	a	c	(a)	b	(d)	△a	□b	52
CTR C-29	a	c	(d)	b	c	(c)	d	a	△b	□a	58
CTR C-30	c	c	d	a	b	(d)	a	(c)	△a	□d	64

Code: ◯ = Inference

△ = Another name for the story

▢ = Main idea of the story

68

VOCABULARY CHECK ANSWER KEY
Lessons CTR C-21 to CTR C-30

LESSON NUMBER

PAGE NUMBER

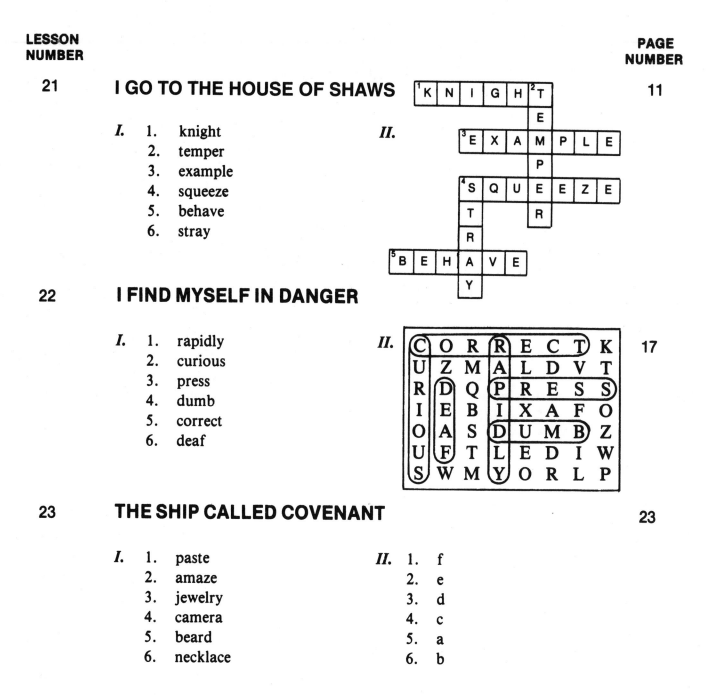

21   **I GO TO THE HOUSE OF SHAWS**   **11**

I.
1. knight
2. temper
3. example
4. squeeze
5. behave
6. stray

II.

22   **I FIND MYSELF IN DANGER**

I.
1. rapidly
2. curious
3. press
4. dumb
5. correct
6. deaf

II.   **17**

23   **THE SHIP CALLED COVENANT**   **23**

I.
1. paste
2. amaze
3. jewelry
4. camera
5. beard
6. necklace

II.
1. f
2. e
3. d
4. c
5. a
6. b

VOCABULARY CHECK ANSWER KEY
Lessons CTR C-21 to CTR C-30

I.
1. keeper
2. season
3. pitcher
4. bargain
5. fortune
6. deserve

II.
1. d
2. f
3. a
4. b
5. c
6. e

I.
1. flap
2. astonished
3. heavens
4. beauty
5. cardboard
6. cereal

II.
1. flap
2. cardboard
3. cereal
4. astonished
5. heavens
6. beauty

I.
1. birth
2. willing
3. divide
4. switch
5. cozy
6. simple

II.
1. False
2. False
3. True
4. False
5. True
6. True

LESSON NUMBER

PAGE NUMBER

27 ALAN AND I ESCAPE IN THE HEATHER   47

I.
1. bedroom
2. note
3. lovely
4. brick
5. twice
6 clothing

II.
1. b
2. c
3. a
4. d
5. b
6. c

28 CLUNY'S CAGE   53

I.
1. inquire
2. coward
3. sore
4. faithful
5. gaze
6. impossible

II.
1. gaze
2. inquire
3. coward
4. faithful
5. sore
6. impossible

29 MY JOURNEY TO MR. RANKEILLOR   59

I.
1. recognize
2. complain
3. message
4. content
5. route
6. greedy

II.

			¹M			
		²G R E E D Y	
³R		E	
E		S	
⁴C O M P L A I N
O		G	
G		E	
N	⁵R	
I	O	
Z	U	
⁶C O N T E N T
	E	

71

VOCABULARY CHECK ANSWER KEY
Lessons CTR C-21 to CTR C-30

30   **I COME TO OWN WHAT IS MINE**   65

I.
1. average
2. copy
3. pitch
4. butcher
5. selfish
6. loft

II.
1. False
2. False
3. True
4. True
5. False
6. False